STUDY GUIDE

Everything in Christ

Paul's Letter to the Colossians

Joel Kim

LIGONIER MINISTRIES
Renew your Mind.
LIGONIER.ORG | 800-435-4343

421 Ligonier Court, Sanford, FL 32771
Email: info@ligonier.org

Printed in China.

Contents

Introduction

Sometimes we might question whether Jesus is enough. This is not a new question, but it is one with a definitive answer. The Colossian church needed a response to false teaching that denied the sufficiency of Christ, and Paul answered with a letter that exalted Christ as the Lord of creation and redemption. Christ is preeminent in all things, which means that Christians lack nothing. In this series, Rev. Joel Kim walks us through Paul's letter to the Colossians so we might embrace all that is already ours in Christ.

This study guide is a companion to the video teaching series. Whether you are using the DVDs, streaming the videos on Ligonier.org, or going through the course in Ligonier Connect, this resource is designed to help you make the most of the learning experience. For each message in the series, there is a corresponding lesson in this guide. Here is what you will find in each lesson:

INTRODUCTION	The introduction is a brief paragraph that summarizes the content covered in the lecture and considered in the study guide lesson. **How to use:** Use the introduction to each lesson to get a sense of the big picture before watching the video. Refer to these statements as you work through the study guide to remind yourself of what you have already covered and where you are headed.
LEARNING GOALS	The learning goals are the knowledge and skills the study guide lesson will endeavor to equip you with as you work through the lecture content. **How to use:** Familiarize yourself with the goals of each lesson before engaging with its contents. Keeping the overall purpose in mind as you watch each video and reflect on or discuss the questions will help you get the most out of each lesson.
KEY IDEAS	The key ideas are the major points or takeaways from the lecture. **How to use:** Use these ideas to prepare yourself for each lesson and to review previous lessons. They describe specifically the knowledge each lecture is communicating.

REFLECTION & DISCUSSION QUESTIONS	The questions are the guided reflection and/or discussion component of the lesson that are intended to help you prepare for, process, and organize what you are learning. **How to use:** Reflect on individually or discuss in a group the questions in the order in which they appear in the lesson. The time stamps in the right margin indicate where the answers to questions during the video can be found.
PRAYER	The prayer section offers suggestions for how to close the lesson in prayer with respect to what was taught in the lecture. **How to use:** Consider using each lesson's prayer section as a guide to personal or group prayer. These sections follow the ACTS prayer model, which you can learn more about in R.C. Sproul's Crucial Questions booklet *Does Prayer Change Things?* This helpful guide is available as a free e-book at Ligonier.org.
REVIEW QUIZ	The review quiz is a set of six multiple-choice questions that appears at the end of each lesson. **How to use:** Use each quiz to check your comprehension and memory of the major points covered in each lecture. It will be most beneficial to your learning if you take a lesson's quiz either sometime between lessons or just before you begin the next lesson in the study guide.
ANSWER KEY	The answer key provides explanations for the reflection and discussion questions and answers to the multiple-choice questions in the review quiz. **How to use:** Use the answer key to check your own answers or when you do not know the answer. Note: Do not give in too quickly; struggling for a few moments to recall an answer reinforces it in your mind.

Study Schedules

The following table suggests four plans for working through the *Everything in Christ* video teaching series and this companion study guide. Whether you are going through this series on your own or with a group, these schedules should help you plan your study path.

	Extended 10-Week Plan	Standard 8-Week Plan	Abbreviated 4-Week Plan	Intensive 3-Week Plan
Week	**Lesson**			
1	*	1	1 & 2	1–3
2	1	2	3 & 4	4–5
3	2	3	5 & 6	6–8
4	3	4	7 & 8	
5	4	5		
6	5	6		
7	6	7		
8	7	8		
9	8			
10	*			

* For these weeks, rather than completing lessons, spend your time discussing and praying about your learning goals for the study (the first week) and the most valuable takeaways from the study (the last week).

1

Jesus Christ Is Lord

INTRODUCTION

The Apostle Paul wrote to the Colossians to encourage them with a simple truth: Jesus Christ is Lord, and He is enough. As Jesus is Lord of both creation and redemption, we must trust that He is all we need and walk in a manner worthy of Him. In this lesson, Rev. Kim addresses how the lordship of Christ is central to Paul's message in his letter to the Colossians. The opening to this book of Colossians lays out a rich understanding of the sufficiency of Christ.

LEARNING GOALS

When you have finished this lesson, you should be able to:

- Explain what Paul means when he declares that "Jesus Christ is Lord"
- Describe what it looks like to walk in a manner worthy of the Lord

KEY IDEAS

- We do not need to add to Jesus' work, because Jesus is enough.
- Jesus is enough because He is Lord over creation and redemption.
- Since Jesus is Lord, Christians ought to walk in a manner worthy of Him.
- Belonging to Jesus Christ changes how we approach the shifting circumstances of our lives.

REFLECTION & DISCUSSION QUESTIONS

Before the Video

What Do You Think?

Take a moment to answer the following questions. They will prepare you for the lecture.

- In what ways do you notice yourself or others trying to add to Christ as if He were not enough?

- How does your identity in Christ and the fact that you belong to Jesus Christ affect the way you live?

Scripture Reading

If you confess with your mouth that Jesus is Lord and believe in your heart that God raised him from the dead, you will be saved. For with the heart one believes and is justified, and with the mouth one confesses and is saved. For with the heart one believes and is justified, and with the mouth one confesses and is saved... For there is no distinction between Jew and Greek; for the same Lord is Lord of all, bestowing his riches on all who call on him. For "everyone who calls on the name of the Lord will be saved."

—Romans 10:9–10, 12–13

- How does Paul describe the lordship of Christ in these verses?

During the Video

Answer the following questions while you watch the video. They will guide you through the lecture.

Jesus Christ Is Lord *0:00–16:57*

- What challenges did the church in Colossae face?

- What message does Paul have for a church struggling to remain faithful to the teachings it received?

- What is Jesus Christ Lord over?

Walking in a Worthy Manner *16:57–24:22*

- What does it mean to live a life worthy of the Lord?

- Who is the One ultimately accomplishing those things that characterize a life worthy of the Lord?

- What characteristic is a mark of maturity in believers?

After the Video

Answer the following questions after you have finished the lecture. They will help you identify and summarize the major points.

- Why is Jesus Christ enough? What actions reveal that a person does not believe this?

  If you are in a group, have the members discuss the ways that our actions flow from our beliefs. It's probably rare for a person to outwardly state, "Jesus is not enough," but deep down, they can hold on to this false belief. We can know this through our actions. Have the group identify actions that may reflect a deeper belief that Jesus is not sufficient.

- How is Jesus Christ Lord over creation and redemption?

  If you are in a group, have the members name various ways that Jesus is Lord over both creation and redemption. Ask: Which passages of Scripture come to mind in support of Christ's total lordship over all things?

- Rev. Kim states that a key theme in Colossians is "our God is wise, good, and powerful, and Christ is your Lord." How does this truth transform how we approach difficulties in life?

  If you are in a group, encourage members to be open with one another. Help them connect over their current struggles and help them to draw encouragement from the work of the Spirit in their lives.

PRAYER

Commit what you have learned from God's Word to prayer.

- Praise God for providing a Savior who is all-sufficient.
- Confess the ways that you do not walk in a manner worthy of Christ.
- Thank God for making the incarnate Son the Lord over all creation and redemption.

- Ask God to help you trust Jesus more deeply, knowing that He is enough, not attempting to add to or take away from His work.

REVIEW QUIZ

Use these multiple-choice questions to evaluate what you learned from this lesson.

1. What is one of the primary issues that Paul addresses in the opening of Colossians?
   a. Purity laws
   b. Circumcision and false teaching
   c. Identity in Christ
   d. Justification by faith alone
2. What summarizes Paul's primary message for the church as it struggles to remain faithful?
   a. Jesus loves you.
   b. You should love Jesus.
   c. Jesus is everlasting.
   d. Jesus is enough.
3. What does it mean that Jesus is Lord of creation?
   a. He created all things.
   b. He created physical things.
   c. He created spiritual things.
   d. All of the above
4. What does it mean that Jesus is Lord of redemption?
   a. Jesus did what He could to help His people.
   b. Jesus is better than the Old Testament sacrifices.
   c. Jesus is the full expression of God's love.
   d. Jesus saved His people and makes them new.
5. In the "openings" to Paul's letters, he often lists the primary theme or issue he plans to address.
   a. True
   b. False
6. According to Paul, what does thankfulness mark in a believer's life?
   a. Genuine gratitude
   b. True faith
   c. Holy works
   d. Christian maturity

Answer Key—Jesus Christ Is Lord

REFLECTION & DISCUSSION QUESTIONS

Before the Video

What Do You Think?

These are personal questions. The answers should be based on your own knowledge and experience.

Scripture Reading

- How does Paul describe the lordship of Christ in these verses?

  Salvation depends on the outward, verbal confession that Jesus Christ is Lord. It's inherent to the Christian faith. There is a connection between belief and confession. One is inward; the other is outward. Saving faith requires inward faith that expresses itself in outward actions. Additionally, Paul highlights Jesus' lordship over all people. He is Lord over Jews and Greeks. He is Lord over the nations. Everyone who calls on Him will be saved and blessed.

During the Video

Jesus Christ Is Lord

- What challenges did the church in Colossae face?

  The church in Colossae was facing challenges from within and without. Paul was in prison at this time, and there were likely local pressures seeking to harm and disadvantage Christians. There were also issues from within, such as false teaching, judgment, and dissensions (e.g., Col. 2:16–18).

- What message does Paul have for a church struggling to remain faithful to the teachings it received?

  Paul's message to the church is that Jesus is enough. When they are tempted to add to Christ by believing something additional or to add specific actions to earn salvation, Paul wants them to know that Jesus is enough. When there are issues that would challenge their competency and they feel inadequate, they need to remember that Jesus is enough. The reason that He is enough is because He is Lord over all things.

- What is Jesus Christ Lord over?

  Jesus Christ is Lord over creation and re-creation. He made all things, visible and invisible. He is also the One through whom redemption comes. He is the One who reconciles a broken and sinful world back to God. In this way, He is the Lord over creation and re-creation, or redemption.

Walking in a Worthy Manner

- What does it mean to live a life worthy of the Lord?

  Many circumstances will challenge our faith in Christ. Wars, famines, politics, economics, hardships, and other trials can cause us to doubt the lordship of Christ. Walking in a worthy manner is not a one-time event; it's a journey through a lifetime. In every situation where we are tempted to doubt the lordship of Christ, walking in a worthy manner means deepening our trust in Him as we are rooted, built up, established in faith, and abounding in thanksgiving.

- Who is the One ultimately accomplishing those things that characterize a life worthy of the Lord?

  It is the Holy Spirit who accomplishes these things. It is the work of Christ in us through the Spirit that causes us to be rooted, built up, established, and abounding in thanksgiving. We are passive recipients of these divine actions as we walk with Christ through our lifetime.

- What characteristic is a mark of maturity in believers?

  Thankfulness is a mark of maturity in believers. This is because we realize that Jesus is Lord and that we are not; He is the One who is doing the things that Paul asks for in Colossians 1:9–12—in and for us. Therefore, our only right response is thankfulness to God.

After the Video

- Why is Jesus Christ enough? What actions reveal that a person does not believe this?

  Jesus Christ is enough because He is Lord over creation and redemption. He is the One who has accomplished everything for us. The actions that reveal a person does not believe that Jesus is enough either attempt to add to His work or take away from it. We add to it by thinking that we can earn God's favor by the things we do or refrain from doing. Often, moral behaviors are attempts at adding to Christ's finished work, even if they are good and biblical things. If people are not rooted in the reality that Jesus Christ alone is the foundation of salvation, then moral behaviors of any kind can be an attempt to earn God's favor. We can take away from Jesus' work when we doubt His forgiveness, love, and favor. In those actions, we show that we do not fully believe that He is enough.

- How is Jesus Christ Lord over creation and redemption?

  To say that Jesus Christ is not Lord over those things would imply that He did not accomplish them. He is the Creator of all things visible and invisible. Everything was created through Him and for Him. Therefore, He is the Lord of creation. Similarly, Jesus accomplished salvation. It came through Him and for Him. He took on flesh. He fulfilled all righteousness and died to pay for the sins of His people, satisfying the wrath of God. He was raised from the dead to defeat death and to secure eternal life for His people. Our salvation is now complete because of His work. In Jesus' ascension, He is enthroned as Lord over all. He is the firstborn of creation, having preeminence over everything.

- Rev. Kim states that a key theme in Colossians is "our God is wise, good, and powerful, and Christ is your Lord." How does this truth transform how we approach difficulties in life?

  Jesus is supreme—He holds all things together by the word of His power (see Col. 1:17). It's a matter not only of believing the truths about Christ Jesus but also of knowing and living in the truth that we belong to Him, forever united to Him, and transformed by Him for His glory. Even on the days when we feel lost, powerless, incompetent, and insecure, we are at that moment being built up by Christ Jesus. We are a work in progress, and Christ is certainly at work within us. What He began by grace, He will finish by grace. Paul emphasizes this elsewhere in his epistle to the Philippians: "I am sure of this, that he who began a good work in you will bring it to completion at the day of Christ Jesus" (Phil. 1:6).

- At the end of the lecture, Rev. Kim explained several ways that describe what it means to live with Christ as Lord. Which of these is most encouraging to you right now? Why?

  These answers should reflect your own personal views and experiences. The four ways that describe what it means to live with Christ Jesus as Lord are being rooted in Him, being built up in Him, being established in the faith by Him, and living in thanksgiving for Him.

REVIEW QUIZ

1. **C.**
   Rev. Kim highlighted that, grammatically, Paul's opening statement reflects a mirroring phrase highlighting his call to those who are in Colossae to live faithfully in Christ. He is addressing their core identity as those united to Christ.

2. **D.**
   "Jesus is enough" is a key theme of the book of Colossians. Paul highlights this on the basis of Jesus' lordship. Since Jesus is Lord over creation and re-creation, the Colossians need to see that Jesus is enough, despite the false teaching or challenges they face.

3. **D.**
   Colossians 1 specifically states that Jesus created everything visible and invisible. Since all things were made through Him and for Him, He is the Lord of all *creation.*

4. **D.**
   Jesus accomplished salvation for His people, and thus, He saved them. He is the Lord of redemption, for not only does He redeem His people from the power and

penalty of sin, but He is also delivering them from its presence. As Lord of creation and re-creation, Jesus is making creation new through His restorative, redemptive work.

5. **A.**
   In Paul's letters, he often reveals the primary issue at hand in his opening statement. This is true for Colossians, and Rev. Kim also pointed to the way that Paul did this in Romans and Galatians.

6. **D.**
   The other aspects may be true of a Christian, but according to Paul's logic and Rev. Kim's explanation, the notable mark of maturity in a believer's life is thankfulness. This type of thankfulness comes when you realize that everything is dependent on Christ. He is the One who has accomplished salvation and who brings about restoration for His people. When we grasp that truth by faith, we respond with thanksgiving as recipients of His blessed grace.

2

Praying with Paul

INTRODUCTION

It is common for Christians to struggle in their prayer life. Prayer can feel strange because in the world, maturity is marked by growth in independence. But in the Christian life, maturity is marked by a greater dependence on the Lord. Sometimes, we feel disconnected from God and need guidance. Other times, we disproportionately pray focused on material things in comparison with spiritual blessings, and we can be confused about the purpose of prayer. In this lesson, Rev. Kim examines the Apostle Paul's prayer in Colossians 1, making four observations about prayer to instruct our own pursuit of God in prayer.

LEARNING GOALS

When you have finished this lesson, you should be able to:

- Identify the importance of prayer in the life of a Christian
- Describe the characteristics of a mature prayer life

KEY IDEAS

- Paul prays constantly with thanksgiving because he depends on the Lord and focuses on spiritual blessings found in Jesus Christ.
- Paul prays for the gospel to bear fruit in the lives of the Christians at Colossae so that they would become mature in Christ.
- Paul prays with great confidence because of his secure identity in Christ.

REFLECTION & DISCUSSION QUESTIONS

Before the Video

What Do You Think?

Take a moment to answer the following questions. They will prepare you for the lecture.

- How would you describe the current state of your prayer life?

- What's the most challenging aspect of prayer for you?

Scripture Reading

For this reason I bow my knees before the Father, from whom every family in heaven and on earth is named, that according to the riches of his glory he may grant you to be strengthened with power through his Spirit in your inner being, so that Christ may dwell in your hearts through faith—that you, being rooted and grounded in love, may have strength to comprehend with all the saints what is the breadth and length and height and depth, and to know the love of Christ that surpasses knowledge, that you may be filled with all the fullness of God.

—Ephesians 3:14–19

- What does Paul pray for? What can you learn about prayer based on his example?

During the Video

Answer the following questions while you watch the video. They will guide you through the lecture.

The Importance of Prayer *0:00–7:19*

- What does it mean that Paul was constant in prayer?

- How does Christian maturity differ from worldly maturity?

The Characteristics of Prayer *7:19–24:31*

- What does thankfulness reveal about the heart? What is Paul thankful for?

- What does Paul pray for in relation to the gospel?

- Why is Paul confident in prayer?

After the Video

Answer the following questions after you have finished the lecture. They will help you identify and summarize the major points.

- Why is prayer so important in the Christian life?

  If you are in a group, have the members confess to one another the ways that they struggle being dependent on the Lord. Ask: What are ways that you equate maturity with independence, and how does this challenge a biblical view of Christian maturity?

- How does Paul teach us to pray?

  If you are in a group, have the members describe the four C's of prayer that Rev. Kim highlighted. Ask: Which of these four C's resonates the most with you?

- According to Paul, how can you become more confident in your prayer life?

  If you are in a group, have each member share the reasons that they don't feel confident in their prayer life. Help them see how the gospel addresses those concerns, showing that the redemptive work of Christ brings greater confidence in prayer.

PRAYER

Commit what you have learned from God's Word in this lesson to prayer.

- Praise God for allowing us to grow in dependence on Him through prayer.
- Confess the ways that you neglect prayer and seek to live independently from God.
- Thank God for giving you guidance from His Word for drawing near to Him in prayer.
- Ask God to cause you and others to grow in maturity through the knowledge and love of Christ.

REVIEW QUIZ

Use these multiple-choice questions to measure what you learned from this lesson.

1. When we say Paul was constant in prayer, what does that *not* mean?
   a. He was always having a mystical experience.
   b. He was making an exaggerated point.
   c. He did nothing except pray.
   d. All of the above.

2. What is the mark of maturity for believers as revealed in these verses?
   a. Independence
   b. Faith
   c. Dependence
   d. Hope

3. Rev. Kim said that the things we most frequently give thanks for reveal what?
   a. What we most highly despise
   b. What we most highly value
   c. What we most highly love
   d. What we most highly trust

4. What did Paul give thanks for?
   a. Signs of favor
   b. Signs of love
   c. Signs of grace
   d. Signs of heaven

5. A remarkable characteristic of Paul's prayers is how often he prays for himself.
   a. True
   b. False

6. What gives us confidence in prayer?
   a. Our identity in Christ
   b. Our good behavior
   c. Our correct doctrine
   d. Our growth in knowledge, love, and hope

Answer Key—Praying with Paul

REFLECTION & DISCUSSION QUESTIONS

Before the Video

What Do You Think?

These are personal questions. The answers should be based on your own knowledge and experience.

Scripture Reading

- What does Paul pray for? What can you learn about prayer based on his example?

  Paul prays for the Father to strengthen believers through His Spirit in their inner being. He asks God to cause Christ to dwell in their hearts by faith, so that they would grow in their comprehension of His immeasurable love for them, having been filled with the fullness of God. Paul teaches us that we should be concerned with the spiritual blessings of Christ in our prayers. We should pray for God to make Christ known in deeper ways, so that we can experience and know His love in greater degrees.

During the Video

The Importance of Prayer

- What does it mean that Paul was constant in prayer?

  Paul is constant in prayer in that he occupies a prayerful attitude in all that he does. He is not always in a trance or mystical state. Paul is doing the normal things of life, but he does them with an awareness of God's presence and an active pursuit of Him through prayerful communion.

- How does Christian maturity differ from worldly maturity?

  Christian maturity is fundamentally different because Christianity has a completely different value system than the world. In the world, maturity is often distinguished by degrees of independence. The more independent you are, the more mature you are. But this is not the case in Christianity, because we are made to be dependent on God. Therefore, the more mature we are, the more we depend on the Lord in prayer.

The Characteristics of Prayer

- What does thankfulness reveal about the heart? What is Paul thankful for?

  Thankfulness reveals what you value. The things that you are thankful for are often the things that occupy your attention. When you are not thankful for something, it is likely that you did not value the thing that was given or the service that was rendered. So what we are thankful for reveals the motives and desires of our heart. Paul displays his heart by giving thanks for the faith of the Colossians in his prayers rather than focusing on lesser things.

- What does Paul pray for in relation to the gospel?

  Paul prays for Christians to grow in maturity. He asks God to give the Colossians the knowledge of Christ, to grow them in faith, hope, and love, and to grow in fuller measures of the Spirit so they can live a life worthy of the Lord.

- Why is Paul confident in prayer?

  Paul is confident in prayer because of his identity in Christ. Jesus died for him and set him apart as holy. Trusting in his Creator and Redeemer, Paul has confident access to approach the throne of grace. This is because of what Jesus has done for him and who Jesus is to him.

After the Video

- Why is prayer so important in the Christian life?

  Prayer is important in the Christian life because it is a distinguished marker of maturity. All Christians go through trials in their prayer lives, and there are some seasons when we do not pray as we should. Prayer, however, is the purest and most active expression of relational dependence in the Christian worldview.

- How does Paul teach us to pray?

  Paul's prayers highlight several aspects of godly prayer. Rev. Kim summarized these with four C's: constancy, characteristic, content, and confidence. Paul's constancy in prayer teaches us how we should depend on the Lord in all things; it's a heart posture, not necessarily a list of things to do. Because we value certain things, we need to reorient our values. What we are thankful for in prayer is a direct reflection of our deepest values. Additionally, Paul's prayer teaches us that we should pray for people to grow in maturity through spiritual grace. All this is possible because of what Jesus had done for Paul, as he had received a new identity.

- According to Paul, how can you become more confident in your prayer life?

  According to Paul, the way to become more confident in your prayer life is to deepen your awareness of your identity in Christ. The more you know yourself to be a sinner saved by sovereign mercy, the greater confidence you will have. As you receive and rest in Christ alone as He is offered in the gospel, you will grow in your experience of this wonderful reality—approaching the throne of grace with confidence.

REVIEW QUIZ

1. **D.**
   This question is clarifying what is not *meant by Paul's constancy in prayer. Paul was not constantly having a mystical experience, nor was he enclosed in a room doing nothing but praying. He also was not exaggerating a point for the Colossians to make them feel a certain way. Rather, Paul's expression about being constant in prayer reflects his posture toward all of life. In all that he did, Paul did it with a posture of prayerful dependence on God.*

2. **C.**
   The mark of maturity revealed in these verses is dependence. Rev. Kim directly stated that independence is a way that the world measures maturity, but this should not be so in the church. As Christians grow in maturity, they grow in their dependence on the Lord. This dependence expresses itself in prayer.

3. **B.**
   Whatever fills your mind the most is what you value most. If something does not regularly come to mind, it is likely not very valuable to you. Rev. Kim made this point in the lecture, illustrating the reality that what we give thanks for is a direct reflection of what we value. If we primarily pray about material things (or if we neglect to pray for spiritual realities), that likely reveals that material things are our highest values.

4. **C.**
   Although each of these can be reflected in the life of a Christian, Paul expressed his thanks for the signs of grace in the Colossians. For Paul, the signs of grace are faith, hope, and love. Since these qualities were exhibited in the believers at Colossae, Paul gave thanks to God. These characteristics are fruit of the gospel, showcasing God's work by the Spirit in their lives.

5. **B.**
   It is actually the opposite. It's striking how Paul prays so frequently for others in his prayers. These prayers are directed to God on behalf of others, and he is concerned for their spiritual well-being above all else.

6. **A.**
   Rev. Kim highlighted identity in Christ as the primary thing that gave Paul confidence in prayer. Paul understood that Jesus died for him and redeemed him from his sin. In confidence and joy, therefore, he comes before the Father as one fully forgiven and accepted in Christ.

3

Theological Doxology

INTRODUCTION

Theology reflects our understanding of who God is and what He has done. Doxology is our worship and praise of God. The two must not be separated. In the same way that you cannot have un-theological doxology—which is idolatry—theology without doxology is stale, empty, and full of unbelief. Paul always holds theology and doxology together, and they mutually build on each other. Knowing and engaging the true God in Christ occurs through theological doxology. Jesus is at the center of our theology and doxology. In this lesson, Rev. Kim explains why theological doxology is necessary and how Christ Jesus is at the foundation of both.

LEARNING GOALS

When you have finished this lesson, you should be able to:

- Articulate what is meant by theological doxology and why it is essential
- Explain how Christ Jesus is at the center of our theology and doxology

KEY IDEAS

- True worship must be informed by theology, and true theology always leads to worship.
- The cause of our thankful praise is our deliverance from sin and the domain of darkness.
- Christ Jesus is the preeminent Lord who has delivered us and redeemed us.

REFLECTION & DISCUSSION QUESTIONS

Before the Video

What Do You Think?

Take a moment to answer the following questions. They will prepare you for the lecture.

- Do you think praising God or knowing God is more important? Explain your answer.

- Is your heart engaged when you study theology or read Scripture? How can you tell?

Scripture Reading

And when he had taken the scroll, the four living creatures and the twenty-four elders fell down before the Lamb. . . . And they sang a new song, saying, "Worthy are you to take the scroll and to open its seals, for you were slain, and by your blood you ransomed people for God from every tribe and language and people and nation, and you have made them a kingdom and priests to our God, and they shall reign on earth. . . . Worthy is the Lamb who was slain, to receive power and wealth and wisdom and might and honor and glory and blessing!"

—Revelation 5:8–10, 12

- In this heavenly praise of Christ, what is He being praised for? What do you think this reveals about true doxology and worship?

During the Video

Answer the following questions while you watch the video. They will guide you through the lecture.

A Song of Thanksgiving *0:00–12:08*

- What is the relationship between theology and doxology?

- What is the inheritance that we have as people of God?

- What is the source of our thankfulness?

A Song About Christ Jesus *12:08–26:10*

- How is Christ preeminent in creation?

- How is Christ preeminent in salvation?

- What does Paul's reflection on the person and work of Christ lead him to?

After the Video

Answer the following questions after you have finished the lecture. They will help you identify and summarize the major points.

- What is meant by theological doxology? Why is it essential?

  If you are in a group, have the members share their experiences of un-theological doxology and un-doxological theology.

- How does this section of Colossians reveal the true source of Christian doxology and thankfulness?

  If you are in a group, have the members share about times they were prompted to be thankful. Ask: How often did their thanksgiving look different from their non-Christian friends or family? Help them ponder what is distinct about Christian thanksgiving.

- Why does Christianity focus so centrally on Jesus Christ?

  If you are in a group, have the members discuss their understanding of who Christ is. Help them see that one's view of and relationship to Jesus is the most important thing about them. Have them reflect on the degree to which they (or their church) focus on things that distract from the centrality of Jesus Christ.

PRAYER

Commit what you have learned from God's Word in this lesson to prayer.

- Praise Christ for His preeminence in creation and redemption.
- Confess the ways that you neglect theological doxology as the central aspect of your life with God.

- Thank God for delivering you from the domain of darkness and sin through Jesus Christ.
- Ask God to continue revealing the riches of Christ to you that you would be filled with wonder and praise.

REVIEW QUIZ

Use these multiple-choice questions to measure what you learned from this lesson.

1. According to this passage, what two things should never be separated in the Christian life?
   a. Love and hope
   b. Sin and salvation
   c. Faith and grace
   d. Theology and doxology
2. What is one central characteristic that is lacking from the false religion Paul addresses?
   a. Love
   b. Thankfulness
   c. Worship
   d. Devotion
3. What is the spiritual inheritance of believers in the Old and New Testaments?
   a. The land
   b. Heaven
   c. God
   d. Salvation
4. What word does Paul use to express the preeminence of Christ?
   a. Creation
   b. Rulers and authorities
   c. Resurrection
   d. Firstborn
5. Jesus' resurrection ensures that all Christians will experience resurrection.
   a. True
   b. False
6. Which theologian was quoted as stressing the importance of theology and worship for seminarians?
   a. Athanasius
   b. John Calvin
   c. B.B. Warfield
   d. Charles Hodge

Answer Key—Theological Doxology

REFLECTION & DISCUSSION QUESTIONS

Before the Video

What Do You Think?

These are personal questions. The answers should be based on your own knowledge and experience.

Scripture Reading

- In this heavenly praise of Christ, what is He being praised for? What do you think this reveals about true doxology and worship?

  Jesus is being praised for His worthiness to open the scroll and bring about God's plan of redemption for all time. The basis of His worthiness is that He was slain, and by His blood, He ransomed a people for God from all nations. He made them priests to God. The Lamb accomplished salvation for His people, and this is the basis of the heavenly saints' doxology. This reveals that true doxology flows from true theology that sees Christ as preeminent in redemption—supreme in all things.

During the Video

A Song of Thanksgiving

- What is the relationship between theology and doxology?

  In Christianity, theology and doxology must be bound together. Un-theological doxology is idolatry. Un-doxological theology is stale and full of unbelief. True theology will always lead to worship and praise because it is about God and His redemption through Jesus Christ, the worthy One.

- What is the inheritance that we have as people of God?

  In the Old Testament, the inheritance began as the literal land, but a shift takes place in Scripture to highlight that the land was a pointer to the deeper inheritance, which is God Himself (see Ps. 16). This becomes the theme of the New Testament in Christ.

- What is the source of our thankfulness?

  The source of our thankfulness is our deliverance from the domain of darkness and sin. This is how Christian thankfulness is unique. Christian thankfulness does not merely thank God for the tangible blessings we have in this life. Christian thankfulness expresses deep gratitude to God for the spiritual blessings we have in Christ, through our redemption that He alone accomplished.

A Song About Christ Jesus

- How is Christ preeminent in creation?

  Christ is preeminent in creation because He is the Creator of everything. All things were created through Him and for Him. He created everything visible and invisible. All authorities came from Him. He is the preeminent One through whom all things were created and through whom all things are sustained. This is because He is the image of the invisible God, the eternal Son of God.

- How is Christ preeminent in salvation?

  Christ is preeminent in salvation because of His resurrection. He has defeated sin, death, and Satan, thus delivering His people from the domain of darkness. His resurrection is the source of our salvation, and He is the standard to which all the redeemed are being molded (see Rom. 8:29).

- What does Paul's reflection on the person and work of Christ lead him to?

  Paul's reflection on Christ led him to doxological praise. He transitioned to a song of praise for the One who is preeminent as Creator and Redeemer. He was led into theological doxology.

After the Video

- What is meant by theological doxology? Why is it essential?

  When we identify theological doxology, we are describing true Christian worship. Anything that is not theological doxology is not wholehearted Christian worship. Theological doxology identifies two potential errors that reflect one's idolatry or unbelief. Un-theological doxology is offering worship to God in a way that isn't formed by true theology. This is the essence of idolatry. According to the Bible, just because someone is spiritual and worshipful does not mean that they are pleasing to Jesus Christ. Doxology must be accompanied by true theology, which centers on the person and work of Christ. Similarly, the second error reflects unbelief. When a person engages true theology without doxology, something is inherently wrong. If you study the truths about Christ and are not prompted to worship and awe, this reflects a hard heart rooted in unbelief.

- How does this section of Colossians reveal the true source of Christian doxology and thankfulness? Why?

  The true source of Christian worship and thankfulness is Jesus Christ—who He is and what He has done. This is found in Colossians' hymn of thanksgiving: Christ is the image of the invisible God, the eternal Son of God. He is the firstborn of creation and redemption, which means He is preeminent in both of those things. He created all things, and He also authored re-creation in redemption. There is no hope apart from Him, and since Christians have been delivered from the domain of darkness, their deliverance in Christ is the source of their thankfulness.

- Why does Christianity focus so centrally on Jesus?

  Christianity focuses centrally on Jesus Christ because He is the eternal Son of God who created and redeemed the world. He existed eternally as the second person of the Trinity, and through Him, the Father created the world. He was not created; He was eternally begotten. This is who He is, and He is preeminent over creation. He is also the means by which salvation occurs. Through Him, the Father redeemed His people from their sin and darkness. There is no way to God apart from Jesus. Everything Christianity teaches centers on Him.

REVIEW QUIZ

1. **D.**
   Although every other answer is true, they are matters of theology. This lesson emphasized the need for theology to lead to doxology and for doxology to be informed by theology. These are the two things that should never be separated in the Christian life.

2. **B.**
   Rev. Kim mentioned that Paul is addressing a false religion in the book of Colossians. Thankfulness is a central characteristic for him to determine true Christianity from false Christianity, because the Colossian heresy was marked by asceticism and rigid devotion. It notably lacked the overflow of a heart of thankfulness as a key component.

3. **C.**
   Even in the Old Testament, God was the inheritance of His people. Psalm 16 expresses, "You are my portion" (v. 5). The good news and hope of the Bible is that we get God Himself as our everlasting inheritance. This is His promise to us.

4. **D.**
   Paul uses all of the concepts listed in these answers to describe Christ's preeminence, but the word he uses to communicate this concept is firstborn. *Jesus is the firstborn of all creation, and He is the firstborn from the dead. Those two statements capture His lordship over all things—creation and redemption.*

5. **A.**
   Indeed, we will experience the resurrection because, as believers, we are united to Jesus Christ by the Holy Spirit. As the firstborn, Jesus ensures that all after Him will experience the same thing. His resurrection is the down payment or firstfruits of salvation for those who believe.

6. **C.**
   The theologian who discussed this concept was B.B. Warfield. Rev. Kim quoted him at the end of the lecture. Warfield was speaking primarily to theologians and seminarians when he raised the question, "Can a religious man stand in the presence of God and not worship?" This question is a worthy one for all Christians to consider in their walk with God.

4

Participation in Christ's Ministry

INTRODUCTION

Ministry is difficult. Many pastors experience burnout, and this is not a new phenomenon. Ministers of Christ have always experienced various degrees of suffering. This was certainly true of Paul. He wanted the Colossians to know that his sufferings did not invalidate the gospel he proclaimed. Rather, he wanted them to see that through his sufferings, God's calling, message, and strength could be clearly seen. In this lesson, Rev. Kim focuses on the nature of participating in Christ's work this side of glory by showing how Christians are experiential participants in Christ's own ministry.

LEARNING GOALS

When you have finished this lesson, you should be able to:

- Explain what Paul was called to do as a minister of Christ
- Clarify how Paul was enabled to fulfill his calling to proclaim Christ

KEY IDEAS

- Paul was called by God to become a minister of Christ.
- As a minister of Christ, Paul's fundamental message was the revealed mystery of Christ.
- Paul was strengthened by the death-defeating power of God to endure the sufferings of ministry.

REFLECTION & DISCUSSION QUESTIONS

Before the Video

What Do You Think?

Take a moment to answer the following questions. They will prepare you for the lecture.

- How does your culture typically view weakness?

- How should a Christian think about suffering?

Scripture Reading

Five times I received at the hands of the Jews the forty lashes less one. Three times I was beaten with rods. Once I was stoned. Three times I was shipwrecked; a night and a day I was adrift at sea; on frequent journeys, in danger from rivers, danger from robbers, danger from my own people, danger from Gentiles, danger in the city, danger in the wilderness, danger at sea, danger from false brothers; in toil and hardship, through many a sleepless night, in hunger and thirst, often without food, in cold and exposure. And, apart from other things, there is the daily pressure on me of my anxiety for all the churches. . . . But he said to me, "My grace is sufficient for you, for my power is made perfect in weakness." Therefore I will boast all the more gladly of my weaknesses, so that the power of Christ may rest upon me. For the sake of Christ, then, I am content with weaknesses, insults, hardships, persecutions, and calamities. For when I am weak, then I am strong.

—2 Corinthians 11:24–28; 12:9–10

- In these verses, what does Paul teach us about weakness and suffering in the Christian life?

During the Video

Answer the following questions while you watch the video. They will guide you through the lecture.

Paul's Calling and Message 0:00–16:30

- Why was Paul an Apostle?

- What is Paul called to do, according to this section of Colossians?

- What fundamental message must Paul preach?

Paul's Strength and Suffering *16:30–23:57*

- What kind of power gives Paul strength?

- What are the sufferings of Paul associated with?

- How does Paul's message reframe the way that Christians should view suffering?

After the Video

Answer the following questions after you have finished the lecture. They will help you identify and summarize the major points.

- What is implicit in the idea of being called by God?

  If you are in a group, have the members discuss Paul's calling and how that shapes our understanding of our own callings.

- Why is it enough that we preach Jesus Christ?

  If you are in a group, have the members talk about their experiences in churches where Jesus Christ was not preached (if they have them). Have them also consider their current church setting and help them come up with ways to pray for and encourage their current pastor(s) as they preach the gospel.

- In what ways are you weak? What sufferings are you experiencing? How do you rely on the strength of God?

  If you are in a group, consider opening up and sharing first as the leader. Share areas where you are weak. If you need examples, look back at the passage from 2 Corinthians 11 where Paul lists his sufferings. This may help encourage openness. Help your group connect their sufferings to the hope of the gospel.

PRAYER

Commit what you have learned from God's Word in this lesson to prayer.

- Praise God for His power that is manifested in our faith-filled weakness.
- Confess the ways that you have tried to strive in your own strength in the Christian life.
- Thank God for the elders and deacons in your church.
- Ask God to strengthen you and help you understand the greater purpose in your suffering as a Christian.

REVIEW QUIZ

Use these multiple-choice questions to measure what you learned from this lesson.

1. According to Colossians, why does Paul rejoice in his sufferings?
   a. God uses them for good.
   b. They complete what is lacking in Christ's redemptive work.
   c. They fill up what is lacking in Christ's afflictions.
   d. They fill up the bowl of God's wrath toward this world.

2. The afflictions of Colossians 1:24 relate to Christ's redemptive sufferings.
   a. True
   b. False

3. How did Paul become an Apostle?
   a. He repented and chose to be one.
   b. God agreed with him that he should go preach to the gentiles.
   c. God called him to be one.
   d. Peter called him and anointed him.

4. What was Paul called to do?
   a. To proclaim the answer to a mystery
   b. To preach Christ
   c. To make the Word of God fully known
   d. All of the above

5. The power working in Christ was the same power working in Paul.
   a. True
   b. False

6. What are Paul's sufferings in ministry associated with?
   a. The mission of Satan
   b. The ministry of Christ
   c. The death of Christ
   d. None of the above

Answer Key—Participation in Christ's Ministry

REFLECTION & DISCUSSION QUESTIONS

Before the Video

What Do You Think?

These are personal questions. The answers should be based on your own knowledge and experience.

Scripture Reading

- What does Paul teach us about weakness and suffering in the Christian life?

  Paul lists a variety of situations in which he had suffered. Some were direct acts of persecution. Others were disruptions to plans, and some were the challenge of lacking provisions. Some of his difficulties were even related to the normal stresses and anxieties that flow from care and concern for loved ones. In all of these things, Paul identifies them as his weaknesses. Paul had learned from Jesus that His grace is sufficient for Paul's weakness. Therefore, Paul boasted in his weaknesses, because he was then boasting in the resurrection power of Christ.

During the Video

Paul's Calling and Message

- Why was Paul an Apostle?

  Paul did not choose to become an Apostle; God divinely chose him. Paul was only an Apostle because of God's grace. Paul did not even ask for God's grace. In fact, he was a persecutor of the church before his conversion. If it were not for God's powerful work in him, Paul would not have become a Christian, much less an Apostle.

- What is Paul called to do, according to this section of Colossians?

  Paul was called to be a steward of the mysteries of God. He was charged with proclaiming and making known fully the Word of God. Colossians 1:25–26: "I became a minister according to the stewardship from God that was given to me for you, to make the word of God fully known, the mystery hidden for ages and generations but now revealed to his saints."

- What fundamental message must Paul preach?

  The message that Paul preached was Christ. He was a Christ-centered preacher. This is because Jesus is the key to unlocking the Scriptures. The Old Testament looks forward to Him and proclaims His coming in a shadowed and mysterious way. The New Testament declares the coming of Christ with great clarity. The messenger of God must preach Christ in order to make known the Word of God fully. This is why Paul says, "Him we proclaim" (Col. 1:28).

Paul's Strength and Suffering

- What kind of power gives Paul strength?

  The same power that raised Jesus from the dead is the power at work in Paul. He was empowered by the Holy Spirit. This is the only way to be strengthened for ministry and the only way to be strengthened in the Christian life.

- What are the sufferings of Paul associated with?

  The sufferings of Paul are associated with the ministry of Christ. They are not contributing to the redemptive work of Christ, as if it were incomplete. Rather, Christians get to actively participate in the life that Christ lived, and their life is now marked by His. Therefore, they experience suffering. This comes from being associated with His ministry, which follows the pattern of suffering and death before glory.

- How does Paul's message reframe the way that Christians should view suffering?

  When Christians suffer, they are filling up what is lacking in Christ's afflictions. These are not redemptive afflictions. Since we are united to Christ, our suffering as His body is His suffering. This is particularly true for those in ministry. Ministers fill up what is lacking in Christ's afflictions as they suffer for the body. They are being used by Christ to build His church, so their life will be patterned after His. The church should take encouragement from this and give thanks for their pastors. They likewise should encourage them. In all our suffering, we ought to rejoice that Christ's power is made perfect in our weakness. In God's economy, this weakness turns out to be our great strength as we rely on Him.

After the Video

- What is implicit in the idea of being called by God?

  This calling means that God is in control, and you are responding to His prompting. Although this lesson highlights the uniqueness of being called to ministry, there are various types of callings. The Reformation reclaimed the notion that all callings are equally dignified. Christians can glorify God in their secular vocations, and He is pleased with their work. Regarding the call to ministry, Paul explained how he was called by God to be in service to Christ. His mission was to make known the Word of God fully. The calling of a minister is to be Word-focused; Paul did this by preaching Christ.

- Why is it enough that we preach Jesus Christ?

  If we are preaching something other than Christ, we are not preaching the gospel.

Therefore, we are not preaching the Word of God. If we are not preaching the Word of God, then we are failing at the call to ministry. Jesus Christ is the mystery of the Old Testament. Everything it says points forward to Him. You can only understand the fullness of the Old Testament's message if you read it through the lens of Christ's person and work. Therefore, it is enough that we preach Jesus Christ because that is the central point of all of Scripture.

- In what ways are you weak? What sufferings are you experiencing? How are you relying on the strength of God?

  The answer to these questions will be personal and unique to each individual, but we do well to remember Christ's words to Paul: "My grace is sufficient for you, for my power is made perfect in weakness" (2 Cor. 12:9).

REVIEW QUIZ

1. **C.**
   In Colossians 1:24, Paul says, "Now I rejoice in my sufferings for your sake, and in my flesh I am filling up what is lacking in Christ's afflictions for the sake of his body, that is, the church."

2. **B.**
   In Colossians 1:24, Paul is not speaking of any deficiencies in the redemptive suffering of Christ. He is also not talking about additions to the work of Christ as if it were insufficient. Paul uses different words in context ("afflictions" for Christ but "sufferings" for himself). These are afflictions associated with an active participation in the ongoing work of Christ this side of glory.

3. **C.**
   While Paul was on the Damascus road attempting to imprison Christians, Christ made Himself known through a vision. He called Paul to Himself, and He gave him the task of being the Apostle to the gentiles. God called Paul according to His perfect will, not Paul's own worthiness.

4. **D.**
   Because he was chiefly tasked with making the Word of God fully known (Col. 1:25), Paul must proclaim Christ. For Christ is the One who unlocks the mystery of Scripture. It is all about Him.

5. **A.**
   According to Scripture, the same power working in Paul was the power that raised Jesus from the dead. It is the power of God at work in Paul to teach in all wisdom and present the church as fully mature. Paul writes, "For this I toil, struggling with all his energy that powerfully works within me" (Col. 1:29).

6. **B.**
   The sufferings of Paul in his ministry are associated with the ministry of Christ. As Paul says, "I am filling up what is lacking in Christ's afflictions for the sake of

His body" (Col. 1:24). But just as the church experiences the affliction of Christ, Christ's power is made manifest in the church's weakness for His glory.

5

The Sufficiency of Christ

INTRODUCTION

The church in Colossae was threatened by false teaching that rejected the sufficiency of Christ. Often, suffering can cause us to question whether or not Jesus is enough for us. Our weaknesses can even be the reason our enemies revile us in an attempt to discredit Christ. Paul experienced these trials, and he concluded that Jesus Christ was enough for him. It is the very essence of the gospel that he preached. In this lesson, Rev. Kim shows how Jesus Christ is sufficient for our weaknesses, most especially for our right standing with God.

LEARNING GOALS

When you have finished this lesson, you should be able to:

- Explain how Christ sufficiently provides for you in your suffering
- Describe how the false teachers in the Colossian church denied the sufficiency of Christ

KEY IDEAS

- Suffering highlights the weakness of the messenger but points to the sufficiency of the Savior.
- Jesus is sufficient for all your spiritual needs.
- Do not be taken captive by any empty philosophy or false teaching that regards Christ as not enough.

REFLECTION & DISCUSSION QUESTIONS

Before the Video

What Do You Think?

Take a moment to answer the following questions. They will prepare you for the lecture.

- How would you summarize Christianity to a non-Christian?
- How do you grow in your faith?

Scripture Reading

I am astonished that you are so quickly deserting him who called you in the grace of Christ and are turning to a different gospel—not that there is another one, but there are some who trouble you and want to distort the gospel of Christ. But even if we or an angel from heaven should preach to you a gospel contrary to the one we preached to you, let him be accursed. As we have said before, so now I say again: If anyone is preaching to you a gospel contrary to the one you received, let him be accursed.

—Galatians 1:6–9

- What is a different gospel? What is the consequence of turning aside to a different gospel?

During the Video

Answer the following questions while you watch the video. They will guide you through the lecture.

Joy in Suffering *0:00–8:19*

- What reason does Rev. Kim give for why Paul could rejoice in the midst of his suffering?
- What does suffering highlight?
- According to 2 Corinthians 1, what benefit comes from suffering?

Jesus Is Enough *8:19–26:10*

- What false belief about Christ arose in the Colossian church?
- What did Paul mean by empty philosophy and deceit?
- What is asceticism?

After the Video

Answer the following questions after you have finished the lecture. They will help you identify and summarize the major points.

- How can the suffering of Christians glorify Christ?

  If you are in a group, have the members describe a type of suffering they experienced that God later enabled them to use to encourage a brother or sister in Christ who was experiencing a similar trial. Reflect together on 2 Corinthians 1:3–5.
- Why did the Colossian church need Paul to remind them that Christ was sufficient?

  If you are in a group, have the members discuss the various aspects of the empty philosophy that Paul described. Ask: Do you hear this type of thinking anywhere today?
- What are some ways that you are tempted to think or believe Christ is not enough?

  If you are in a group, have each member share the struggles of their heart in relation to trusting Christ completely. Ask: In what area of your life do you doubt His sufficiency?

PRAYER

Commit what you have learned from God's Word in this lesson to prayer.

- Praise God that Christ is all-sufficient.
- Confess ways that you are tempted to turn to another gospel and act as if Christ were not enough.
- Thank God for using your sufferings to bring glory to Christ and draw you nearer to Him.

- Ask God to give you opportunities to encourage others with the comfort that you have received from Him.

REVIEW QUIZ

Use these multiple-choice questions to measure what you learned from this lesson.

1. How did Paul's opponents view his suffering?
   a. As a benefit
   b. As a mockery
   c. As a blessing
   d. As a weakness
2. In our suffering, what does the world see?
   a. We are not the Messiah.
   b. We are unworthy.
   c. We have it all together.
   d. We love weakness.
3. Which of the following was *not* a lesson taught by Rev. Kim, regarding the role of suffering for a Christian?
   a. It highlights the weakness of the Savior.
   b. It highlights the weakness of the messenger.
   c. It shows the messenger that it is not about him.
   d. It forces him to rest in the sufficiency of Christ alone.
4. Which command does Paul give in Colossians?
   a. Do not let anyone take you captive.
   b. Do not let anyone pass judgment on you.
   c. Do not let anyone disqualify you.
   d. All of the above
5. Paul was criticizing the study of philosophy.
   a. True
   b. False
6. Which of the following best describes asceticism?
   a. Doing what you want
   b. Changing your behavior to fit in
   c. Restricting the desires of the body
   d. Giving in to the desires of the body

Answer Key—The Sufficiency of Christ

REFLECTION & DISCUSSION QUESTIONS

Before the Video

What Do You Think?

These are personal questions. The answers should be based on your own knowledge and experience.

Scripture Reading

- What is the consequence of turning aside to a different gospel? What is a different gospel?

  According to Paul, the consequence is being cursed. Jesus Christ is the only hope for sinners, and the gospel is the declaration that salvation is found in Him alone. There can be many different seemingly competing "gospel" messages. In his letter to the Galatians, Paul describes the doctrine of justification in great detail. He argues that it is the essence of the gospel that God declares us righteous in Christ alone by faith alone and not by our works. An overemphasis on works-based righteousness, as was encountered in Galatia, is a different gospel. The danger of a different gospel could also be found in Colossae.

During the Video

Joy in Suffering

- What reason does Rev. Kim give for why Paul could rejoice in the midst of his suffering?

  At the beginning of the lecture, Rev. Kim mentions that it's because Paul knows and rests on the promises of God—that He will never leave him nor forsake him. That promise was very real to Paul, and this truth is how Paul could rejoice in the midst of his suffering.

- What does suffering highlight?

  Suffering highlights our weakness, but it points to the strength and sufficiency of the Savior. It also reminds the messenger of the gospel that everything is not about him. It is a great honor to suffer for something that is greater than ourselves. It causes us to be utterly dependent on the sufficiency of Christ as we participate in the sufferings of Christ. In this way, our suffering magnifies His grace and glory.

- According to 2 Corinthians 1, what benefit comes from suffering?

  There are two benefits of suffering, according to 2 Corinthians 1:3–5. First, God will comfort you in your suffering. Christ draws near to the brokenhearted.

He knows how to comfort the afflicted, because He Himself was afflicted and comforted by the Father. Second, after being comforted by the Father through Christ, Christians learn how to comfort others. In God's providence, He will cause you to encounter people experiencing similar struggles to what you have faced, and He will enable you to comfort them with the same comfort that you received.

Jesus Is Enough

- What false belief about Christ arose in the Colossian church?

  The false belief was that Jesus was not enough. This came about through the erroneous teaching that was an empty philosophy, full of deception. It attempted to bring judgment on believers. It did so by requiring them to merit the fullness of God's favor and therefore disqualifying them from it. Such teaching taught that the way to please God was through asceticism, and the core of the teaching denied the sufficiency of Christ.

- What did Paul mean by "empty philosophy and deceit"?

  The false teachers presented something that sounded plausible from a worldly perspective but was not in accord with the gospel. Therefore, it was deceptive. It was also a teaching that was empty, in that it had no power. It did not point to the truth, nor could it attain the truth. Paul was not criticizing the general concept of philosophy as much as he was warning about letting our minds be captivated by empty and deceptive truth claims from false teachers.

- What is asceticism?

  Asceticism is the denial of one's bodily urges, desires, or needs. There are various forms of it, and Paul mentions a few: "do not touch," "do not taste," and so on. They may have the appearance of wisdom, but they have no power to position us in a better relationship with God. This is not what God wants from us. It is simply worldly wisdom based on the foundational principles of the world that is opposed to godliness.

After the Video

- How can the suffering of Christians glorify Christ?

  The suffering of Christians can glorify Christ because it serves as a sign that points to Him. If Christians would be more open about their suffering, it would serve as an opportunity to bring glory to Jesus. This is because one's weakness highlights the sufficiency of the Savior. It shows that it is not our strength that serves as the basis of our relationship with God; it's our trust in Christ, who alone is strong. This is the type of Savior every person needs.

- Why did the Colossian church need Paul to remind them that Christ was sufficient?

  They needed Paul to remind them of Jesus' sufficiency because there were false teachers that were attempting to take their minds captive with an empty philosophy that was deceptive. They started embracing asceticism as a way to qualify themselves for salvation. This denied the reality that the Father alone has "qualified [them] to share in the inheritance of the saints in light" (Col. 1:12). God did this definitively when He "delivered [them] from the domain of darkness and transferred [them] to the kingdom of his beloved Son, in whom we have redemption, the forgiveness of sins" (Col. 1:13–14). It was Paul's primary aim to restore them to these realities that were already theirs in Christ.

- What are some ways that you are tempted to think or believe Christ is not enough?

  The answers will be unique to each individual, but many times we struggle with the same temptations. We can have a tendency to look to our own performance for a sense that we are right with God or we can seek comfort apart from God, adding to Christ instead of depending solely on Him.

REVIEW QUIZ

1. **D.**
   In both Colossians and his letters to the Corinthians, Paul's opponents viewed his suffering as a weakness. It was as if they were asking: "If he was such a great Apostle, why was he in jail? Why was he beaten so many times? Would God not deliver him if Paul were His Apostle?" The false teachers attempted to use Paul's weakness as a way to disqualify him. In response, Paul pushed back and showed how his weakness was the validating feature of his ministry.

2. **A.**
   One of the good things about suffering is that it shows we are not the Messiah, that we are not the Christ. He is the One who is the Savior, and He alone is sufficient. In ourselves, we are not sufficient. Our suffering and weakness function as a sign pointing others to the all-sufficient Savior.

3. **A.**
   Rev. Kim gave four reasons that suffering benefits the Christian, but our suffering does not reflect the weakness of our Savior; rather, it highlights His sufficiency to save those who are weak. When it comes to our salvation, none of us are strong enough to save ourselves. We all need a strong Savior.

4. **D.**
   Each of these statements is made by Paul to the Colossians. Rev. Kim clarified that what is notable in this section of Colossians are the negative commands that Paul gives.

5. **B.**
   Even though Paul said, "Do not let anyone take you captive to empty philosophy or deceit," he was not criticizing the study of philosophy itself. He was merely highlighting the danger of embracing a worldview that denies the sufficiency of Christ.

6. **C.**

   Asceticism is the restriction of bodily desires. It is the denial of what you want and what is most natural. Often, you deny what is needful. The practice is a form of legalism that makes people believe that God is pleased with them only when they deny themselves in these ways. Underneath this practice is the belief that "Christ is not enough."

6

Homesick for Christ

INTRODUCTION

One of the remarkable claims of the New Testament is that Christians are spiritually united to Christ. This union is distinguished by belonging. We are no longer our own; we belong to Christ. This is not simply a future hope for believers—we experience this reality now. In Colossians, Paul reminds Christians of these truths, and he calls them to set their minds on things above where Christ is. In this lesson, Rev. Kim explains how union with Christ ought to remind us that this is not our home. Belonging to Christ transforms the way that we live our lives on earth.

LEARNING GOALS

When you have finished this lesson, you should be able to:

- Explain what is meant by union with Christ
- Discern what it looks like to yearn for heaven as your true home

KEY IDEAS

- Christians are spiritually united to Christ and belong to Him.
- A Christian's identity and value stem from their union with Christ.
- Christians are to focus on an eternal perspective rather than just the present moment.

REFLECTION & DISCUSSION QUESTIONS

Before the Video

What Do You Think?

Take a moment to answer the following questions. They will prepare you for the lecture.

- Do you remember a time when you were homesick? What prompted that feeling, and what was the experience like?

- How might the concept of homesickness relate to our faith in Christ?

Scripture Reading

"I do not ask for these only, but also for those who will believe in me through their word, that they may all be one, just as you, Father, are in me, and I in you, that they also may be in us, so that the world may believe that you have sent me. The glory that you have given me I have given to them, that they may be one even as we are one, I in them and you in me, that they may become perfectly one, so that the world may know that you sent me and loved them even as you loved me. Father, I desire that they also, whom you have given me, may be with me where I am, to see my glory that you have given me because you loved me before the foundation of the world."

—John 17:20–24

- What does Jesus pray for regarding unity, oneness, and presence?

During the Video

Answer the following questions while you watch the video. They will guide you through the lecture.

Union with Christ *0:00–15:06*

- What is the first and foremost message that Paul is communicating in Colossians 3:1–4 about how to live as a Christian?

- What does union with Christ mean for our identity?

- When does this union take place?

Living with Homesickness *15:06–24:05*

- What does it mean to be an alien or pilgrim?

- What characterizes us as sojourners and pilgrims?

- Since Christ is your life, what should that life be characterized by?

After the Video

Answer the following questions after you have finished the lecture. They will help you identify and summarize the major points.

- How should a Christian think about their relationship with Jesus Christ?

  If you are in a group, have the members discuss some of the ways that Rev. Kim explained union with Christ. Encourage them to share things that stood out as new, surprising, or helpful.

- What are some ways that meditating on your union with Christ can encourage you in your faith?

  If you are in a group, have the members reflect on and share times when they either felt like they didn't belong or had no value. Help them get to an honest answer by beginning the conversation and sharing your own experience.

- What does it look like for a Christian to set his mind on things above where Christ is?

  If you are in a group, have each member share where they struggle with worldliness. Ask: What aspects of your life are overly focused on the here and now? How can the doctrine of union with Christ change this perspective?

PRAYER

Commit what you have learned from God's Word in this lesson to prayer.

- Praise God for His abundant generosity in uniting His people to Himself through Christ.
- Confess ways that your mind is set on things on earth rather than on things in heaven.

- Thank God that, if you are united to Christ, Jesus Christ is your life and that your life is hidden in Him.
- Ask God to help you see yourself in terms of your union with Christ so you might have a heavenly homesickness for Him.

REVIEW QUIZ

Use these multiple-choice questions to measure what you learned from this lesson.

1. Where is a Christian's citizenship?
   a. Earth
   b. All nations
   c. Church
   d. Heaven
2. The phrases "in Him" or "with Him" are a shorthand for what concept?
   a. Being together with Christ and united to Him
   b. Having Him live in your heart
   c. Believing in Him
   d. Both b and c
3. According to Rev. Kim, belonging to Jesus affects your what?
   a. Success
   b. Value
   c. Identity
   d. Both b and c
4. What word captures the idea that the "future is already here" for Christians?
   a. Eschatological
   b. Already–not yet
   c. Christian futurism
   d. Premillennialism
5. Christians should celebrate now because they fully possess Christ.
   a. True
   b. False
6. The heavenly-minded life recognizes the difference between what two concepts?
   a. Grace and gratitude
   b. Godlessness and goodness
   c. The godward life and the earthbound life
   d. The godly life and the good life

Answer Key—Homesick for Christ

REFLECTION & DISCUSSION QUESTIONS

Before the Video

What Do You Think?

These are personal questions. The answers should be based on your own knowledge and experience.

Scripture Reading

- What does Jesus pray for regarding unity, oneness, and presence?

  Jesus prays for believers to experience oneness and unity in Him. This is more than merely agreeing about things. He is praying that they will experience a substantive oneness that reflects the oneness between the Father and the Son. Additionally, Jesus prays that they would be one with Him and the Father. This is a prayer for union with Christ. Jesus brings about our union with Himself through His effectual prayer as the High Priest. In that union, He prays that believers would experience a real presence with Him.

During the Video

Union with Christ

- What is the first and foremost message that Paul is communicating in Colossians 3:1–4 about how to live as a Christian?

  The first and foremost message of Colossians 3:1–4 is that Christians belong to Jesus Christ. They are His. Rev. Kim paraphrased it this way: "You need to remember these things in order for you to daily carry on your life following Christ Jesus, that first you belong to Christ."

- What does our union with Christ mean for our identity?

  It means that whatever happened to Him has vicariously happened to us. He died, so we died. He was raised, so we were raised. He is in the presence of the Father, so we are in the presence of the Father. Because we are united to Him, we have great value. He is the source of our value. When we begin seeing who we are in these terms, our faith is fueled and strengthened, and our minds are set on things above.

- When does this union take place?

  This union takes place now. It is also a future reality. We have it in part now, but we will experience it fully in the future. This is described as a semi-eschatological state or something already–not yet. We already are united to Christ, and we experience real benefits from that, but we are not yet experiencing the fullness of those benefits.

Living with Homesickness

- What does it mean to be an alien or pilgrim?

  To be an alien or pilgrim means that you are residing in a place that is not your home. Rev. Kim told a story about being a Korean-American as an example of this. These terms are used to describe citizenship relative to the place where one finds himself, and they are often used to describe the Christian life on this side of glory.

- What characterizes us as sojourners and pilgrims?

  Christ characterizes us. Paul says that Christ is our life. Because we are citizens of heaven, we possess heavenly DNA, and thus, we love differently and have a different demeanor than the world.

- Since Christ is our life, what should our life look like?

  Since Christ is our life, our life should be characterized by valuing things of eternal consequence rather than focusing on the temporal here and now. It should include a different value system that is not based on this world's ways. The world's values become flipped, such that meekness is strength and loss is gain. Essentially, our life should look like life in the kingdom of God (see Matt. 5:1–12).

After the Video

- How should a Christian think about their relationship with Jesus Christ?

  They should think of themselves as united to Christ. This requires setting your mind on things above. Union with Christ emphasizes the way that you belong to Him. You are with Him in heaven. Therefore, heaven is where your citizenship resides. Christians should see themselves so deeply united to Christ that what happened to Him also vicariously happened to them. They experience the benefits of salvation by being united to Christ, the One who accomplished the work of salvation. Thus, they have great value, for they are one with the eternal Son of God. Regardless of what the world thinks about them, they possess an identity that cannot be diminished.

- What are some ways that meditating on your union with Christ can encourage you in your faith?

  Primarily, your answers should be personal and will vary, but here are some questions to consider further: (1) When you sin, in what ways do you doubt God's love for you? (2) In what circumstances do you tend to feel as if God has abandoned you? (3) In what ways do you derive value from your successes and accomplishments? (4) What would it look like to have your identity and value resting in Christ?

- What does it look like for a Christian to set his mind on things above where Christ is?

  When a Christian sets his mind on the things above, he will experience longing and homesickness for heaven. Rather than focusing on the instant gratification of this life, we focus on the eternal realities related to Jesus Christ and His Kingdom. Our value system will reflect Christ's rather than the world's, and we will see our identity and value stemming directly from our union with Him.

REVIEW QUIZ

1. **D.**
   In many ways, this is the message of the entire lecture. A Christian's citizenship resides in heaven. This is because of our union with Christ. Therefore, we should be homesick for heaven. It's why Paul calls us to set our minds on things above.

2. **A.**
   These phrases occur more than 160 times in the New Testament. They are shorthand phrases for describing our union with Christ. When he died, we died. When He was raised, we were raised. When He ascended, so did we. Christians are those who are united to Him, those who are "in Christ."

3. **D.**
   During the lecture, Rev. Kim discussed the ways that the world focuses on our success. From these worldly successes, we derive our identity and value. As Christians, our union with Christ is the basis for our value and identity. These should be the things that ground us by faith and give us assurance of value and not worldly success and accomplishment.

4. **B.**
   For Christians, our life in Christ is possessed in an already–not-yet way. It is ours—we are seated with Him in heavenly places—but we do not know this reality fully until we are with Christ in glory.

5. **B.**
   Christians should celebrate now because they belong to Christ. But this statement is false because of one word: fully. *We do not yet* fully *possess Christ in the sense of being glorified with Him. This is what we ultimately long for.*

6. **D.**
   At the end of the lecture, Rev. Kim described what the life of Christ looked like. He made contrasts between worldly values and kingdom values. He then made this direct statement, "A heavenly-minded life is a life that recognizes the difference between a good life and a godly life."

7

Our Heavenly Accent

INTRODUCTION

Accents often indicate where a person is from. This verbal marker tells a story about an individual's background and context. Since Christians are not of this world, they have a specific accent demonstrated in how they live. It is a heavenly accent because of who they are in Christ. Christians put to death many things in their lives, and other things they actively pursue. Additionally, this accent provides them with the gospel message for the world. In this lesson, Rev. Kim explains how one's heavenly citizenship reveals itself throughout one's life.

LEARNING GOALS

When you have finished this lesson, you should be able to:

- Describe how our identity in Christ forms the way we live
- Explain how our identity in Christ shapes the things that we say

KEY IDEAS

- We have a heavenly accent because of who we are in Christ.
- What we do flows from who we are.
- We ought to pray for open doors to share the Word of God.

REFLECTION & DISCUSSION QUESTIONS

Before the Video

What Do You Think?

Take a moment to answer the following questions. They will prepare you for the lecture.

- What would a heavenly accent "sound" like in someone's life?

- What elements of evangelism are difficult for you?

Scripture Reading

For Christ also suffered once for sins, the righteous for the unrighteous, that he might bring us to God, being put to death in the flesh but made alive in the spirit. . . . Since therefore Christ suffered in the flesh, arm yourselves with the same way of thinking, for whoever has suffered in the flesh has ceased from sin, so as to live for the rest of the time in the flesh no longer for human passions but for the will of God.

—1 Peter 3:18; 4:1–2

- What is the argument behind Peter's command to resist the flesh and live for the will of God?

During the Video

Answer the following questions while you watch the video. They will guide you through the lecture.

A Heavenly Accented Life *0:00–13:41*

- What is the gospel logic found in Paul's writing?

- What imperatives does Paul give in this passage?

- How are we called to live relationally?

A Heavenly Accented Message *13:41–25:37*

- What is another accent that marks the Christian?

- What does the "open door" metaphor mean?

- Who and what is involved in evangelism?

After the Video

Answer the following questions after you have finished the lecture. They will help you identify and summarize the major points.

- How does our heavenly identity in Christ shape our lives?

  If you are in a group, have the members discuss some of the ways that Rev. Kim explained how our heavenly accent is displayed.

- Why is the relationship between who we are and what we do so important?

  If you are in a group, have the members share ways that they have experienced this connection in other areas of life.

- How is evangelism related to having a heavenly accent?

  If you are in a group, have each member share a time when they shared their faith and displayed their identity in Christ. Also have them reflect and share about a time when they had a gospel opportunity and did not take it. Help them frame these as opportunities to demonstrate their heavenly accent in Christ.

PRAYER

Commit what you have learned from God's Word in this lesson to prayer.

- Praise God for giving us a heavenly identity in Christ.
- Confess ways that you do not put your sin to death.
- Thank God for being the One who converts sinners through His Word.
- Ask God for an open door to share the gospel with a non-Christian neighbor.

REVIEW QUIZ

Use these multiple-choice questions to measure what you learned from this lesson.

1. According to this lecture, everyone has a what?
   a. Attitude
   b. Accent
   c. Allergy
   d. God
2. What is an indicative?
   a. A reality that flows from what Christ has done for us
   b. An idea about what we could be
   c. A future state
   d. A command
3. What is an imperative?
   a. A reality that flows from what Christ has done for us
   b. An idea about what we could be
   c. A future state
   d. A command
4. In Christianity, what is the relationship between indicatives and imperatives?
   a. Indicatives follow imperatives.
   b. There is no relationship.
   c. Imperatives lead to indicatives.
   d. Indicatives lead to imperatives.
5. When we covet, we are engaging in idolatry.
   a. True
   b. False
6. What does Paul pray for?
   a. An open door for a platform
   b. An open door for his passion
   c. An open door for the Word
   d. A closed door on sin and Satan

Answer Key—Our Heavenly Accent

REFLECTION & DISCUSSION QUESTIONS

Before the Video

What Do You Think?

These are personal questions. The answers should be based on your own knowledge and experience.

Scripture Reading

- What is the argument behind Peter's command to resist the flesh and live for the will of God?

  Peter's argument is that we are united to Christ, and so we should follow His path. Since He suffered for sins and after being put to death in the flesh was made alive in the Spirit, we should also put to death our flesh and live by the Spirit. We live not for human passions but for the will of God. This occurs when we are made alive by the Spirit and do not gratify the desires of our flesh.

During the Video

A Heavenly Accented Life

- What is the gospel logic found in Paul?

  Paul's gospel logic is that who you are determines what you do. Your identity precedes your behavior. For Christians, their union with Christ is the grounds for putting sin to death and living for Him.

- What are the imperatives that Paul gives in this passage?

  Paul tells the Colossians to put to death sexual immorality and other things that serve as replacement gods. Additionally, he commands Christians to put away behaviors that corrupt and inhibit the Christian community. We are supposed to love one another and be clothed in humility, gentleness, and the various fruits of the Spirit.

- How are we called to live relationally?

  We should put on love, patience, kindness, goodness, and self-control. We are to encourage one another in the Word, and we are supposed to guard the way that we speak.

A Heavenly Accented Message

- What is another accent that marks the Christian?

  Another heavenly accent that Paul highlights is prayer—specifically, prayer for evangelism. Those who are from the heavenly city desire to share that city with others, so they pray for the opportunity to share the gospel.

- What does the "open door" metaphor mean?

  The metaphor of open doors in the ancient world communicates ready access. For a door to be open meant that a person had access to whatever was on the other side. Paul prayed for open doors to proclaim the Word.

- Who and what is involved in evangelism?

  Paul prayed for God to be the One who would open the doors. It was completely dependent on Him. Not only was He the One to open the door, but He was also the One who gave the message. It was His Word going forth that Paul prayed for.

After the Video

- How does our heavenly identity in Christ shape our life?

  This identity shapes our lives because it marks us as His own. We do not live like the rest of the world. Our lives should have a distinctive character to them. They should flow from our identity in Christ. It involves the inner renewal of our desires, so that we do not covet in idolatrous ways. Rather, we are content with our lot, for we trust God and His provision for us. Additionally, we put our sin to death. We put on characteristics of love, compassion, self-control, and patience. We should also be marked by prayer and evangelism.

- Why is the relationship between who we are and what we do so important?

  If you reverse this order, it's no longer a Christian way of life. We always receive the gift of our identity before entering into the requirements of God. Jesus has accomplished salvation and provided everything we need to glorify and enjoy Him. Apart from His work in us, we are unable to honor and please Him. Therefore, it is vital to retain the principle of indicatives coming before the imperatives.

- How is evangelism related to having a heavenly accent?

  Having a heavenly accent not only affects what we do and how we speak, it also shapes what we speak about. We want people to know Christ. Paul prayed for the doors to open so that he could share the Word of God. It is God's Word that transforms and convicts sinners. Since we belong in heaven and are called to have a heavenly-mindedness, it makes sense that we should pray for God to save others and provide an opportunity for us to share the gospel.

REVIEW QUIZ

1. **B.**
   Throughout the entirety of the lecture, Rev. Kim used the concept of an accent as an illustration. He wanted us to realize that everyone has an accent, and we as Christians should think of our identity in Christ as giving us a particular accent in

the world. We do not sound like the world because we are no longer from the world. This heavenly accent displays who we are and our story as God's people.

2. **A.**
   An indicative is a truth or reality that describes something. In the Bible, indicatives are the realities that are true for God's people based on what He has done for them. In Colossians, Paul explains that we are redeemed and in Christ.

3. **D.**
   An imperative is a command. It's a direction for what to do. They can be positive (i.e., do this) or negative (i.e., do not do this).

4. **D.**
   This relationship is vital to understand. Indicatives precede imperatives. In other words, God gives you an identity and accomplishes something for you before giving you a command. He changes who you are before telling you what to do. For example, He unites you to Christ and seats you with Him in the heavenly places, and then He tells you to keep your mind on things above and to put sin to death.

5. **A.**
   Paul highlights this in Colossians 3:5. Our covetousness often leads us to commit other sins. Underneath our coveting is an idol. The things that we covet, in some sense, become our god.

6. **C.**
   Paul prays that God would give him an open door for the Word. It is God who opens the door, and it is God's Word that Paul desires to go through the door. This is instructive to us for our own prayers and evangelism.

8

Ministry, Partnership, and Friendship

INTRODUCTION

The primary theme in the book of Colossians is that Jesus Christ is enough. The Apostle Paul highlights the sufficiency of Christ again and again as he opposes the false teaching that was threatening to take the church captive. In a letter that emphasizes the sufficiency of Christ, Paul ends in a way that causes us to reflect on our interdependence with others. Paul did not minister alone. He had many friendships and partnerships. In this lesson, Rev. Kim reflects on Paul's interconnectedness among other ministers and highlights the importance of reconciliation between Christians.

LEARNING GOALS

When you have finished this lesson, you should be able to:

- Describe how Paul's ministry was connected with various relationships
- Discuss the significance of the mention of Barnabas and Mark at the end of Colossians

KEY IDEAS

- Paul never ministered alone.
- There are pains that come with working together as Christians.
- The Lord brought reconciliation to Barnabas, Mark, and Paul.

REFLECTION & DISCUSSION QUESTIONS

Before the Video

What Do You Think?

Take a moment to answer the following questions. They will prepare you for the lecture.

- Do you prefer to do things by yourself or work with a team? Why?

- Share about a time you lost a meaningful relationship. If reconciliation occurred, how did it happen, and how did this feel?

Scripture Reading

Let us hold fast the confession of our hope without wavering, for he who promised is faithful. And let us consider how to stir up one another to love and good works, not neglecting to meet together, as is the habit of some, but encouraging one another, and all the more as you see the Day drawing near.

—Hebrews 10:23–25

- According to Hebrews, what is necessary for Christians as they wait for the Lord's return?

During the Video

Answer the following questions while you watch the video. They will guide you through the lecture.

Paul's Friends and Co-Ministers *0:00–15:26*

- Though we're saved by Christ alone, are we supposed to do life alone? How does Paul's life demonstrate an answer to this question?

- Who were some of the people Paul ministered with?

- Is working together easy? Why or why not?

Barnabas and Mark *15:26–26:58*

- Who was Mark?
- Who was Barnabas?
- Why is it significant that Paul mentions them at the end of Colossians?

After the Video

Answer the following questions after you have finished the lecture. They will help you identify and summarize the major points.

- How did Paul do ministry? What does that tell us about the Christian life?

  If you are in a group, have the members try listing all the friends and co-laborers mentioned in the lecture with the idea of highlighting the vast number of connections and friends that were part of Paul's ministry. Ask: Who are your co-laborers?
- What does Paul's reconciliation with Mark and Barnabas reveal about the power of the gospel?

  If you are in a group, have the members share about a relationship in which they need reconciliation or which God powerfully worked to reconcile. Spend time in prayer for those relationships and discuss how this reconciliation between ministry partners is an encouragement.
- What is the most important concept that you have learned in studying the letter of Colossians?

  If you are in a group, have each member identify the most important concept they have learned in this teaching series and discuss the significance of these concepts.

PRAYER

Commit what you have learned from God's Word in this lesson to prayer.

- Praise God for giving us a community in the church.
- Confess ways that you resist reconciliation because of your resistance to confess sin or forgive someone.

- Thank God for providing Christ, who is a sufficient Savior, and for providing fellow Christians for the work of ministry.
- Ask God to grow His church, that many more may labor with us as the body of Christ.

REVIEW QUIZ

Use these multiple-choice questions to measure what you learned from this lesson.

1. Why do the letters of the New Testament often contain personal greetings?
   a. It was the authors' way of communicating.
   b. The people writing and receiving the letter knew each other.
   c. It was a frequent way to bring a letter to an end.
   d. All of the above

2. Paul never did ministry alone.
   a. True
   b. False

3. Doing ministry with others is usually what?
   a. Easy
   b. Relaxed
   c. Simple
   d. None of the above

4. What did Mark do?
   a. Lied to Paul
   b. Got angry
   c. Abandoned Paul
   d. Left Barnabas

5. Most scholars see value in a letter's ending.
   a. True
   b. False

6. Who was Barnabas?
   a. A mature believer and friend of Paul who accompanied him on several journeys
   b. An immature believer who left Paul
   c. A family friend of Mark's
   d. A believer and friend of Paul who accompanied Peter on his journey to Jerusalem

Answer Key—Ministry, Partnership, and Friendship

REFLECTION & DISCUSSION QUESTIONS

Before the Video

What Do You Think?

These are personal questions. The answers should be based on your own knowledge and experience.

Scripture Reading

- According to Hebrews, what is necessary for Christians as they wait for the Lord's return?

  It is necessary for Christians to hold fast to their confession. What we believe matters, and we must finish the race by holding to our confession of faith in Christ. We need to stir others up to faithfulness, and we ourselves need to be stirred up by others. Underlying both of these statements is the need to remain together as a strong community. We do that by regularly meeting together so that we can encourage one another. In other words, we should not walk the Christian life alone. We need others alongside us.

During the Video

Paul's Friends and Co-Ministers

- Though we're saved by Christ alone, are we supposed to do life alone? How does Paul's life demonstrate an answer to this question?

  No. Paul's ministry is marked by deep relationships, and the lesson that Rev. Kim draws out for us is that we need to be connected in the church. Jesus Christ is sufficient for our salvation, but we are not self-sufficient for life.

- Who were some of the people with whom Paul ministered?

  At the end of his letter, Paul gave several personal greetings and mentioned various people who ministered alongside him. He mentioned Tychicus, Onesimus, Aristarchus, Mark, Jesus called Justus, Epaphras, Luke, Demas, Nympha, and Archippus.

- Is working together easy? Why or why not?

  No. It is often complicated. There are various challenges to working with a team. Personality factors can get involved, and oftentimes it seems easier to just continue alone. This was not Paul's method. He worked with people. He did experience the challenges of this collaboration. He persisted with others because it was important to function as the body of Christ. He even lost his best ministry partner, Barnabas, because of a personal conflict and disagreement.

Barnabas and Mark

- Who was Mark?

  Mark was the cousin of Barnabas, and he accompanied Paul on an early missionary journey, but he abandoned Paul and Barnabas. Paul and Barnabas divided because of Mark. Later in his life, Paul was reconciled to Barnabas, and he requested that Mark join him in what he thought would be the final days of his life.

- Who was Barnabas?

  Barnabas was a member of the Jerusalem church. He was a faithful believer and a good man who was full of faith. He became Paul's first ministry partner. He then accompanied Mark after he and Paul split.

- Why is it significant that Paul mentions them at the end of Colossians?

  It is significant that Paul mentions Mark and Barnabas at the end of Colossians because it shows that they experienced reconciliation. Colossians was written after their ministry split, so this is evidence that they were able to experience relational restoration.

After the Video

- How did Paul do ministry? What does that tell us about the Christian life?

  Paul did ministry alongside others. He had deep friendships and partnerships. The list of people included in the ending of his letter shows how connected he was. He knew various people involved at the Colossian church, and he also highlighted the greetings of certain people who were with him. This tells us that Christians should not do life alone. We need one another in the body of Christ. This is true for believers generally, but it's especially true of ministers. They ought not be alone. That was not Paul's method or example.

- What does Paul's reconciliation with Mark and Barnabas reveal about the power of the gospel?

  We are not told the details of what happened. We do not know the conversations that led to their falling out. We also do not know the conversations and interactions that led to their restoration. Other than the places where Paul speaks of them positively at the end of Colossians and 2 Timothy, Scripture is silent on the details of their relationship after their separation in Acts. Their reconciliation, however, shows us that the gospel is powerful enough to heal broken relationships. It may take time, but God is at work, and He can provide reconciliation for believers who have disagreements.

- What is the most important concept that you have learned in studying the letter of Colossians?

  The answer to this question should express what you considered the most important concept that you learned while studying the letter of Colossians. An answer will vary from person to person.

REVIEW QUIZ

1. **D.**
   All these were common reasons for including personal greetings at the end of a letter. This was the means of communication available to them. Therefore, many letters in the New Testament contain personal greetings, and this reflects the communal nature of the first-century church. They knew each other and had relationships with those throughout the Roman Empire.

2. **A.**
   This was a central point from the lecture. Paul ministered together with others. Depending on how one numbers the list, he had roughly eighty or ninety colleagues in ministry. The list of people from Colossians shows that he was connected and not alone in his walk with Christ.

3. **D.**
   Contrary to any of the options listed, doing ministry with others is hard. It's full of difficulty and challenge. There can be personality differences that lead to problems, as well as matters of sin that fracture relationships. Reconciliation is often required, but sometimes, it's a slow process to get there. We see this reflected in Paul's relationship with Mark and Barnabas.

4. **C.**
   Although we do not know why or what all the circumstances involved were, Mark abandoned Paul. Although it is clear that he did not leave the faith, he did leave the missionary journey that Paul and Barnabas were on. He later tried to rejoin them, but Paul did not want him to join them.

5. **B.**
   Unfortunately, many scholars overlook endings as meaningless. They see them as not having much substance to consider relative to the rest of the body of the letter.

6. **A.**
   Rev. Kim highlighted how mature and respected Barnabas was. He sold his property and gave it to the church. He is used in Acts as a counter-example of faithfulness in comparison to Ananias and Sapphira. He went on early journeys with Paul. But he later left Paul to accompany Mark, since he disagreed with Paul.